NLP Excellence

How to become more confident, and convincing in your communication using the science of persuasive words

By John Cassidy-Rice

www.free-nlp.co.uk

Copyright and Legal Information

About the Author

John Cassidy-Rice

John has been involved in NLP and Personal Development for over 15 years. A recognised and certified International Master NLP Trainer. He has become sought after as a Mentor in NLP. He is the co-founder and principle trainer of NLP Excellence running courses on a national and international basis (www.free-nlp.co.uk)

John has a relaxed refreshing humour and informative style. He is adept at using games, models and music to create an environment where learning is easy and fun. He has a reputation for getting results, a deep understanding of how the mind works and how language affects interaction in life.

His trainings are designed to dramatically increase the creativity, teamwork and performance of organisations and individuals through music and learning technologies. He has worked with many companies such as The Financial Times and Accenture. His work has taken him all over the United Kingdom, and also Internationally in Texas and Florida, USA, and Australia.

John is a Managing Partner for the Wizard of Ads, an international marketing company. This involves training, research and consultancy in marketing and advertising. A dynamic public speaker in this area.

Contents

Introduction: Mastering the Language of Influence

One of the most powerful skills in business and in life is the ability to influence others.

Naturally being able to influence others to buy our products, support our proposals or share our point of view is extremely valuable.

But being able to influence ourselves positively in the way we think and act is also important.

The key to influence is language – the words we use and how we use them. But in school, we are only taught part of the story. We usually focus on grammar, spelling and punctuation.

> *"The key to influence is language – the words we use and how we use them."*

But there is usually a much deeper significance to the words we use than the simple dictionary definition.

Neuro-linguistic Programming has built up around the study of the deeper meaning of words and how they influence people to think and act. Studying NLP therefore gives us the expertise to better understand and influence others.

When you can truly understand what other mean when they choose particular words and when you can choose your own words carefully to create the results you want, you can enjoy the real power of influence

The problem is that many people who learn NLP struggle to apply the techniques they have learned in their everyday life.

At the same time, many people would benefit from knowing how to use language to improve their influence skills but hey don't have the time to attend a full training on NLP.

I created this short book to help both groups of people develop the knowledge, techniques and expertise to the Master the Language of Influence.

When you've read this book, you'll have developed the skills of powerful influence.

> *"When you've read this book, you'll have developed skills of powerful influence."*

You'll be able to use this in your private life and in coaching, sales, customer service or any area of business or personal communication to get even more successful results.

To your success
John Cassidy-Rice

# 1.	The Building Blocks of Influential Communication

In this book, we'll go through each of the key elements of the language of influence.

First it's important to understand a few important concepts that will help you make the most of this powerful knowledge.

1. The Science of Neuro-linguistic Programming

Many of the concepts in this book come from the science of Neuro-Linguistic Programming (NLP) so in case you're not familiar with this field, it's important to have a little background.

The two people generally credited with developing NLP are Richard Bandler and John Grinder. Bandler was a psychology student at the University of California at Santa Cruz in 1970, when he joined a group led by Grinder, then an associate professor of linguistics at the school.

The two men became friends and began working together.

They were both impressed with the seemingly magical effect that therapists such as Virginia Satir and Fritz Perls had on their clients and also by the results of Milton Erickson's hypnosis.

They wanted to see if they could break down the process these therapists were using so it could be more easily reproduced by anyone.

Bandler used his background in mathematics and computers and Grinder used his linguistics knowledge to detect patterns and create models.

Over time, NLP has grown in popularity and developed many different strands and has now become as a sort of "open source" system, drawing from many areas of science and psychology.

The patterns of influential language we draw on here owe much to the original studies by Bandler and Grinder as well as other leading figures in the world of NLP.

You do not need to have studied NLP to benefit from this information but the more you study NLP, the better you will be able to apply it in your life.

2. Your attitudes and beliefs about influence

While the language you use is a very important part of your power to influence, there are a few keys to having the right mindset for effective communication.

Here are some key points to bear in mind.

> *"If you are not getting the desired response, you have to do something differently."*

- **You need to recognize and respect the way others see the world:** Before you can influence someone, you need to recognize that they have a different 'model of the world' from you. You need to try to see the world from their viewpoint if you are to influence successfully.

- **There is no failure in communication, only feedback:** whenever you communicate with someone, you will always get some kind of response. It just may not be the one you want right away. They key is to use that response as feedback to help you change rather than to see it as failure.

- **Resistance to communication reflects your inflexibility as communicator:** If you are not getting the desired response, you have to recognize that you need to do something differently. It's amazing how often people keep on doing the same thing even when it doesn't give them the result they want.

- **The meaning of the communication is the response you get:** It can be frustrating if you feel someone is interpreting your message in a different way from what you intend. But you have to make sure that what they hear is what you want them to hear not what you think you said.

- **You must take full responsibility for getting the results you want:** The outcome of any communication is always either the result you wanted or an excuse for why you don't have it. Successful people never have excuses they always do what is necessary to get the result.

3. Your sensory acuity

To influence others, you need to be able to identify whether you are being successful in getting your message across to them.

The key here is that you will not always be able to tell this from their words. You need to be able to interpret their facial expressions, their tone of voice and body language too.

We need to train our minds to focus on these other factors. This ability to observe and interpret the cues that other people give us is called sensory acuity.

The more we can develop our ability to notice these subtle changes, the more easily we can respond to them and therefore improve our ability to influence others.

4. The power of rapport

One of the most important keys to influence is the ability to you're your audience – whether it is one person or thousands – quickly build a feeling of trust and comfort with you.

This state of confidence and trust between two or more people is known as rapport.

Where there is good rapport, people understand each other better and there is more chance of good communication.

> *"Where there is good rapport, there is more chance of good communication."*

Building rapport is a process that happens naturally over time as we get to know and like someone.

One of the keys to getting someone to like you is to help them feel that you are alike in some way.

When you meet someone new, you can speed up this 'liking' process by deliberately 'matching' them in some way – that is by subtly copying something about them – outside of their conscious awareness.

Here are some of the things you can match to build rapport with someone:

- **Words:** Listen to what the other person says and use similar words/phrases in your own communication.

12

- **Physiology:** When you subtly copy the person's posture, hand gestures and movements, they will unconsciously feel that you are like them.

- **Voice:** You should match the tone, tempo and volume of the other person's voice. If they are slow and deliberate, they will feel comfortable if you are the same way.

- **How they deal with information:** Some people like a lot of details while others just want the big picture. You need to give them information in the style they want in order to build rapport.

- **Common experiences:** Identify common experiences or values with the other person and make sure the other person is aware of them.

Where there is good rapport, people understand each other better and there is more chance of good communication.

5. Your congruence

Though language is one of the keys to influence, the impact of your words will depend on whether you deliver them congruently.

If you don't believe what you are saying and don't have confidence in the message, this will show to your audience.

You can look at congruence as 'internal rapport' – a state where you are happy and content with your feelings and thoughts toward a given situation.

In this state, you are comfortable 'in your own skin' and reflect that degree of comfort to the world around you.

When you are in rapport with yourself, you are also more in tune with your audience and better able to interpret feedback and adjust your content so that it is meaningful.

> *"The impact of your words will depend on whether you deliver them congruently."*

In some situations, you may need to learn to appear as if you are congruent even when you have doubts.

You have to deliver your message with conviction.

Even if your statement is not true – or you are not totally convinced – it should be plausible so that people could imagine it being true.

6. Knowing the outcome your want

To ensure your communication is packed with the power of influence, you need to make sure you are clear on the purpose.

When you define clearly the outcome you want from your communication, it is easier to determine exactly what you need to say.

You will also be able to monitor how successful your communication is being and therefore decide what you need to do to change if you are not getting the results that you want.

If you don't have a clear outcome in mind, you won't know whether it is being successful.

Usually you'll want to define the result in terms of action being taken

14

by the other person – it may be them making a purchase or changing their behavior or giving support to something you propose.

Communication that does not have a defined purpose is just chatting.

You need to be clear what you actually want people to do as a result.

7. Being ethical

The language of influence can have very powerful results and gives you a huge advantage over those who don't know it.

So for some this raises questions of ethics.

> *"The language of influence can have very powerful results and gives you a huge advantage."*

The key to ethics is your motivations.

If your intention is to create a false impression so that you get a quick sale or make a fast false impression, this may work in the short-term but it will not be sustainable.

On the other hand, if you want to create a situation where you understand the other person's needs more effectively so that you can serve them better, then you are working in everyone's interests and it will help you be more successful.

Therefore provided your motivation is positive, and that your message is about helping others, you should do everything possible to make your message persuasive and convincing.

15

2. Discover What's Going On In Someone's Mind When You Communicate With Them

In today's instant-response world, we are bombarded with a never-ending stream of constantly-changing information through all of our senses.

As a result, our nervous systems are being subjected to an unimaginable volume of information. The level of data being thrown at the average human mind every day would fill up a computer hard-drive in a few hours.

But fortunately, the human 'computer' has a built-in mechanism for screening information that enables it to cope – otherwise we'd all go crazy.

> *"The level of data thrown daily at the human mind would fill a computer hard-drive in a few hours."*

When you want to influence people, you need to know how this screening process works so that you can get your message across.

NLP Communication Model

One valuable way of understanding this process is known as the NLP Communication Model.

This model helps us understand the steps the mind goes through when somebody notices something – it might be an item they see on television, an email or a comment somebody makes.

Here are some of the steps our minds go through to filter this new piece of information.

16

Deletion, Distortion and Generalization

When we process the information that our senses have taken in, we adapt what we see based on our own experience and priorities.

- When we **delete** information, our mind decides not to make us consciously aware of it.

- If we **distort** information, we change its meaning into something different, based on pre-conceived ideas.

- When we **generalize** information, we put things into convenient categories by saying 'that is the same as ...'

These shortcuts are essential to manage the flow of information but can sometimes work against us. Understanding these tactics the mind uses for processing information will be important in later sections.

Memories and Decisions

When we are choosing whether to pay attention to something, we are heavily influenced by our **memories** of similar events that have happened to us in the past and also by **decisions** we have made in previously.

Values, Beliefs and Attitudes

Our **values** are the feelings that motivate us and help us decide what to do. They guide us when to feel good about something and when to feel bad.

> **"The 'Internal Representation' we create in someone's mind will determine the outcome we get in communication."**

Beliefs are the way we see the world. They act as an 'on/off' switch that can determine what we feel able to do.

Attitudes are our collections of beliefs and values around subjects and will have a big influence on what we do.

Metaprograms

Metaprograms are unconscious filters that have a big impact on the way we think and act. As a result, they are important in determining the differences between people.

For example:

- 'Introverts' typically enjoy their own company when they want to relax while 'extroverts' re-energize in the company of larger groups.

- 'Thinkers' tend to be cool and rational about decisions whereas 'feelers' tend to rely more heavily on their emotions.

Of course, few people are at extreme ends of the scale but most tend to be closer to one of the other.

The mix of our metaprograms explains how two people see the same things differently or why one will buy and the other will run the opposite way.

> **"The mix of our metaprograms explains how two people see the same things differently."**

Understanding your own metaprograms and those of people around you can give you a big advantage in making your communication more influential.

The overall filter process

The result of this filtering process is that we create something inside of our head that is known as an 'Internal Representation'.

18

This may be in the form of a picture, a sound, a feeling, a smell, a taste or words (in the form of self-talk). This all happens very quickly at an unconscious level.

It is the Internal Representation we create that will lead us to make a decision and take a specific action in response to the original event.

The key to being able to persuade people to take the action we want is to influence the Internal Representation they create in their mind. The Internal Representation we create determines the outcome we get.

3. Use All the Senses to Make Your Communication More Successful

We all experience the world around us – and events that happen – through our senses – we may see, hear, touch, smell or taste.

Even inside our mind, our internal representations are held as pictures, sounds, smells or tastes – or they may be words as self-talk.

In communication, the most important sensory categories are described as Visual (sight), Auditory (sound), Kinesthetic (touch or feeling) and Auditory Digital (self-talk).

The key point about senses is that different people pay more attention to one or more of the senses rather than to others.

Understanding this is crucial if you want to make your communication as influential as possible.

> *"People pay more attention to one or more of the senses rather than to others."*

For most people, one of their senses represents their preferred representational system.

The mistake most people make is to communicate using their own preferred system and not taking into account the preferences of their audience.

Depending on the preferred representational system, people will respond differently to different language. For example, some typical words with strong appeal for each category include:

- **Visual**: See, appear, imagine, focused, envision, look, reveal and view.
- **Auditory**: Listen, resonate, sounds, rings a bell, tune in, silence and harmony.
- **Kinesthetic**: Feel, touch, grasp, catch on, make contact, hard, concrete and solid.
- **Auditory Digital**: Sense, experience, understand, think, process, decide and consider.

Few people fall into one of the categories exclusively but usually they have one or two that are dominant.

To maximize your influence, you need to use a variety of words that ensure you have the widest possible appeal.

Use things like "Look at this"; "Does that feel right?" or "Can you hear what I'm saying?"

If you know the preferred system of the person you are talking to (from listening carefully to them) use the words they prefer.

And remember that use of the senses does not just apply to the words.

A visual person will want to have something to look at so they will lose interest if listening only to audio.

Someone who is kinesthetic will want to have something to touch or hold – ideally a sample if you are trying to sell them something.

So, for maximum impact, you need to find ways to represent your message in as many of the modalities as possible.

Influence in Action: Sensory Modalities

Here are some examples of how to use this information in different practical settings.

In Sales and Marketing

Customer says: Can I take a look at some samples of this product?

- o Bad response: I'd be delighted to tell you all the details of our new range.
- o Good response: Let me show you some of these. They look great and I'm sure you'll see something you like.

Describing a new mobile phone

- o Visual: *The layout has a completely new look and you can easily imagine that others will admire it*
- o Auditory: *You may have heard others saying that the sound quality of this model is much better than before*
- o Kinesthetic: *The phone has been designed to fit comfortably into your hand and to make it easy to press the buttons*
- o Auditory Digital: *This new AL579 comes with 24 new features and there is currently a saving of 25% on the price listed in our brochure*
- o Combined: *Take a look at the new AL 579 model and see how comfortable it is when you are talking on the phone. The new design means it fits neatly in your hand. And because of the latest ALB technology - one of the 24 new features – it has the best sound quality ever. And all at 25% off the list price.*

In Management

Boss says: Can you give me a full report with all the details?

- o Bad response: I'll take a look at the big picture and give you my view.
- o Good response: I'll study the facts and prepare a full analysis to help you decide the action needed.

<u>Memo to Employees</u>

- o Visual: *When you take a look at the vision we've revealed today for the business, you'll see that we have a very bright future ahead of us*
- o Auditory: *As you've probably heard, we've been listening to comments about the best way forward for the business and I'm delighted to tell you that we're in a very sound position*
- o Kinesthetic: *I feel very proud to be putting this plan for the future in your hands today. Working hand-in-hand with colleagues, we've been able to grasp the changes that need to be made and now have very firm foundations going forward.*
- o Auditory Digital: *I know you'll be delighted to learn that today we are publishing the detailed implementation plans for the next stage of our growth process. We've paid attention to all the proposals received and, without a doubt, our plans for the future make a lot of sense.*
- o Combined: *Today we are publishing our vision for the future of the business. We've carefully read all your comments and listened to your suggestions. As a result, we've created detailed plans that you'll see put us on a very sound footing going forwards. I'm looking forward to hearing that these changes are catching on very quickly. I'm sure you'll agree they make a lot of sense.*

In Relationships

Partner says: We never see eye to eye, you always seem to take a different view from me.

o   Bad response: You never listen to anything I say. I' feel I'm talking to myself.

o   Good response: Let me show you some of these. They look great and I'm sure you'll see something you like

In Coaching

Note how this example starts by responding to the client using visual language and moves through the other modalities to make specific points and then moves back to visual to finish off.

Look, I can see that you've had a problem facing up to this issue in the past but let's try looking at it from another viewpoint and see if we can paint a picture of how it could seem different in the future.

If I can ask you just to listen for a moment as I tell you a story that I heard recently. I think you'll find that it resonates with you and that the message is as clear as a bell.

This was a guy who felt exactly the same as you but he was able to tap into something different and get hold of the problem and throw it out. If you can make contact with those resources within yourself you'll find you feel totally different.

Can you see that this approach is illuminating and notice how being able to focus like this gives you a much clearer perspective?

Exercise

Consider a communication problem you currently face. Think about the people involved and consider whether changing the sensory language could help you overcome the problem.

4. The Truth Behind the Words: Decode the Real Meaning of the Words Someone Uses

In any statement, there are always certain assumptions lying behind the words that are used.

These assumptions are facts that have to be accepted as true in order to make sense of a statement.

For example, in the statement "the cat came in the door", you have to assume that there is a cat and there is a door.

Obviously in more complicated sentences, there is scope for a more complex series of assumptions and these assumptions are important in communication.

The fact is only part of any communication is carried by the actual words that are used. Much of the meaning is not expressly stated in the words. Rather it is implied in the way those words are put together.

Linguistic presuppositions

The elements of communication which are implied rather than expressly stated are known as presuppositions.

Presuppositions are important in influential communication for two main reasons.

- If we can identify the presuppositions in what someone says, we can identify the person's views in much more detail. If there are many presuppositions in a statement that someone makes, you may have to work harder to change their mind.

- You can actively use presuppositions in your own communication to help influence someone's attitude.

However, to use the full power of presuppositions in influential communication, you have to be able to recognize whether something is a true presupposition or whether it is a mind read.

For example, in the above example, we know there is a cat and there is a door. But if we think the cat is coming in for food, then that is a mind-read or an assumption on our part.

Recognizing presuppositions

We can identify a number of different types of presupposition that can be included in a statement and some of the main ones are as follows.

- **Existence**: Almost every sentence contains a presupposition of existence. You need to look out for a noun or proper noun – including someone's name.

> *"You have to be able to recognize whether something is a true presupposition or a mind read."*

- **Possibility/Necessity**: Here we are looking for verbs which indicate the possibility or necessity of doing something. So look out for words like 'can', 'could' and 'have to'. This also applies negative statements such as 'can't'.

- **Cause and effect**: These presuppositions link one thing to another using words such as 'because', 'If _ then _' and 'Whilst _ then _'. The presupposition assumes a direct relationship between one thing and another. This is used when there is a time lag from one element to the other.

- **Complex equivalence**: Here you are looking for the word 'means' or any variations of the verb 'to be' – am, are. An example is that 'reading this means you are becoming an expert in influential language'. This is used when two things are happening at the same time.

- **Awareness**: This applies to statements using verbs relating to any of the senses – such as seeing, hearing, feeling, tasting.

- **Time**: This relates to use of time words such as 'now', 'stop' or any verb tense that presupposes past, present or future.

Example of Presuppositions

If I wear this suit I will not be allowed into the restaurant.

Here are some of the presuppositions in this statement:
- I exist
- Suits can be worn
- I have the possibility of wearing suits
- I have the possibility of making a decision
- I am going to a restaurant
- This event will happen in the future
- I have the option to make a choice from the range

The simple phrase on its own seems unremarkable but you were probably unaware that you unconsciously accepted several presuppositions within it.

You probably also added a few assumptions of your own about the reasons behind it that are not actually presuppositions.

The key is to be able to notice when others use presuppositions and when to be able to build them into your own communication to make it more influential.

Making Use of Presuppositions

> *"Sometimes you need to loosen up the presupposition before you can make your main point."*

When you hear a presupposition in someone else's statement, it can help you identify you easy it will be to get them to agree with you.

Sometimes you will need to work on loosening up the presupposition inherent in their statement before you can convince them of your main point.

Some of the language patterns we look at in the later sections have the purpose of helping loosen up presuppositions and making people re-evaluate their views.

You can also use these language patterns to build presuppositions into your own communication to make it more likely others will agree with your points.

Influence in Action: Linguistic Presuppositions

Presuppositions are a valuable tool for motivational speakers and for politicians who want to inspire people and give them confidence.

In these opening paragraphs of John F Kennedy's inaugural address as the president of the United States on 20th January 1961, he uses several presuppositions to get people behind his message.

By stacking these presuppositions so early, the audience will more easily accept what he says later.

Text	Presupposition
We observe today not a victory of party but a celebration of freedom--symbolizing an end as well as a beginning--signifying renewal as well as change. For I have sworn before you and Almighty God the same solemn oath our forbears prescribed nearly a century and three-quarters ago.	Existence: If we can observe we must exist – even if you disagree with the message
The world is very different now.	Time: In the course of a few words, we cover the past, present and future
For man holds in his mortal hands the power to abolish all forms of human poverty and all forms of human life. And yet the same revolutionary beliefs for which our forebears fought are still at issue around the globe--the belief that the rights of man come not from the	Possibility: We are opened up to what is possible

generosity of the state but from the hand of God.	
We dare not forget today that we are the heirs of that first revolution.	Necessity: these are our responsibilities
Let the word go forth from this time and place, to friend and foe alike, that the torch has been passed	Awareness: Others can see and hear this for themselves
to a new generation of Americans--born in this century, tempered by war, disciplined by a hard and bitter peace, proud of our ancient heritage--and unwilling to witness or permit the slow undoing of those human rights to which this nation has always been committed, and to which we are committed today at home and around the world. Let every nation know, whether it wishes us well or ill, that we shall pay any price, bear any burden, meet any hardship, support any friend, oppose any foe to assure the survival and the success of liberty. This much we pledge--and more.	Complex Equivalence: because of what we have experienced, we will not allow it to be undone

5. Hypnotic Language: How to Make Sure Your Message Always Gets Through

The originators of NLP – John Grinder and Richard Bandler – were impressed with the results achieved by the American psychiatrist Milton H. Erickson who used hypnosis in his family therapy work.

Perhaps surprisingly, what they discovered about they way he worked as a therapist has become very valuable information for people wanting to communicate persuasively with any audience.

Erickson was widely considered to be the world's greatest medical hypnotist and his work with 'impossible' clients was often seen as 'miraculous'.

So Grinder and Bandler spent a great deal of time studying his methods to see if they could find a pattern to his success.

> *"The Milton Model can be where it is important to communicate directly with the unconscious mind."*

The found that he had a very clear structure to the way he worked and they were able to develop a model based on these studies – which they called the Milton Model.

One of the key things they found was that his key skill in communication with patients was being 'artfully vague'.

He did not believe that direct instructions worked with the unconscious mind and he felt that suggestions had to be more subtle. He said hypnosis worked best when there were gaps in the communication and people had to mentally fill them in from their own experience.

The Milton Model can be used in any kind of communication where it is important to communicate directly with the unconscious mind.

Since successful communication is almost always unconscious, that means it can be applied in most types of communication.

For example, you can use the Milton Model to:

- **Build rapport:** It is easier to build rapport if you keep your language vague. When your language is very specific, you give people more opportunities to disagree with you or reject what you are saying.

- **Communicate persuasively:** When you keep the language vague, you induce a light trance which helps bypass the critical faculties of the conscious mind.

  People fill in the gaps the way they want and therefore are more easily swayed to your viewpoint.

In short, you want to create a situation where the natural result of the communication is that the other person agrees with you.

So you can use the Milton Model to make you language more hypnotic and persuasive.

> **"You can use the Milton Model to make you language more hypnotic and persuasive."**

Let's have a look at the elements of the model and at some examples of you can use these in practice to create language that is ambiguous, hypnotic and enticing.

The Milton Model of Hypnotic Communication

Mind reading

A mind read is where you claim to know what the other person is thinking or feeling without saying how you came by the information.

As you sit there reading this, I know that you're wondering...

Lost performative

A lost performative is a value judgement where the person doing the judging is not specified.

It's a good thing to do this

In this statement, we don't know who says it's a good thing. So we are left to wonder who thinks it's a good thing and maybe why it's a good thing.

Cause and effect

A cause and effect statement claims that one thing causes another.

Reading this will make you more confident in your communication.

Cause and effect statements often use forms such as 'If... Then...', 'Because' or 'Makes'

Even if the cause and effect statement isn't true, it is likely to be accepted by the other person as long as it is plausible.

Complex equivalence

A complex equivalence is a statement where two things are equated. It often uses the word 'means' or a derivative of the verb 'to be'.

The fact you're reading this means you already understand the language of influence.

The complex equivalence doesn't have to be true to be useful as long as it sounds meaningful and plausible.

Universal quantifiers

Universal quantifiers are generalisations used to displace resistance such as 'all', 'everyone', 'nobody', 'one'.

They have no referential index so it's not clear who or what they apply to. They often have an element of exaggeration.

Everyone knows that people who learn to master the language of influence become rich.

A person should never underestimate the power of universal quantifiers!

Presuppositions

We looked at presuppositions in more detail in the previous section. They can be utilised to great effect in hypnotic communication.

Your unconscious mind has already learned more than you realize.

The presuppositions here are that you have an unconscious

mind, it learns and it has already learned something.

Modal operators

Modal operators are words which imply possibility, impossibility or necessity. They tend to define the rules we set in our lives.

It's not impossible to master the language of influence.

This category includes words such as 'must' and 'should' as well as 'can' or 'can't'

Nominalisation

A nominalisation is a process word that has been frozen in time by making it act like a noun even though it is not something tangible.

Reading this will give you many useful learnings

In order to ascribe meaning to the word 'learnings', you have to decide what meanings that word has for you and then map those onto it.

Unspecified verbs

This is where we have a verb that doesn't really tie in with anything else. It's not clear exactly what it means.

He touched her

In this sentence, there is not enough information for us to know exactly what it means – how? where? with what?

The advantage of unspecified verbs in hypnotic communication is that they attract less resistance. The person hearing them makes sense of them using their own model of the world and is therefore more likely to accept the communication.

Unspecified verbs commonly used in hypnotic communication include:

Think, understand, remember, wonder, sense, feel, know, enjoy, learn, travel, recall, discover, move, touch, change and renew.

Tag questions

This is a question placed at the end of a statement and is designed to displace resistance. It moves attention to the question rather than the statement.

So the format for using it is usually a statement then the question.

This is the most valuable thing you can learn. Isn't it?

The aim of the tag question is to have the person showing they agree with you either verbally or non-verbally such as with a nod of the head.

Tag questions are great, aren't they?

Tag questions can also be used in the negative. Can't they?

Lack of referential index

Lack of referential index is a type of generalisation and refers to a phrase which doesn't directly identify a portion of the listener's experience.

In this chapter you will be learning many new things.

When phrases are generalised in this way, they are more likely to fit with the world model of the listener and thus be accepted by the listener.

The above statement is difficult to disagree with and is easy to accept. If the statement was more specific – e.g. in this chapter, you will learn what mind reading is – it would leave room for the reader to decide they don't want to read it.

Comparative deletions

This is where we make a comparison with something, person or standard but the thing to which the comparison is made is not mentioned.

It's better this way

Because of the information that's been deleted, we can neither prove nor disprove the claim made in the comparison.

Pacing current experience

This is where we use words describing what is currently going on around the person. It should utilize different senses.

...and you are here now, reading these words, thinking those thoughts and learning many new things.

The first part of this is an undeniably accurate pace of their current experience so their natural response is agreement.

Even though they may not be learning new things, the pacing statements establish a path of agreement so increase the likelihood they will accept the second part of the statement too.

Double binds

A double bind is a statement which creates the illusion of choice by using the word 'OR' where in fact there is no choice.

Would you like to finish reading this book now OR later?

It doesn't matter which side of the OR you pick, the result will be the same.

This makes it easier for the person to accept your suggestion because they feel at least unconsciously that they are making a choice.

Extended quotes

An extended quote contains the words of a number of people quoting each other so it's not easily to tell where one quotes ends and another starts.

"Many years ago, I was speaking to a friend who told me about a conference he had attended and the speaker mentioned a book he had read where the author said "You should practice hypnotic language every day"."

This approach can make it easier to pass on some information or requests as the message will not be attributed to the immediate speaker. It may not be clear at the time who actually said it but the information will still be heard and accepted unconsciously.

Utilisation

This is where you make use of what is happening or being said to lead back to the outcome you want.

Statement: *"I don't understand."*

Response: *"That's right...you don't understand, yet, because you've not asked the one question that will allow everything to fall into place."*

Because you are using their comments – which are verifiable – they will respond more positively.

Conversational postulates

A conversational postulate is a closed question i.e. one which appears to require a ' Yes' or 'No' response. But instead it causes the listener to perform some action out of their awareness.

'Can you tell me the time?'

Strictly the answer to this question is 'Yes' or 'No' but most people will respond by telling you the time or apologizing if they cannot. People are geared to respond to this as a command even though there is no command there.

This approach allows you to issue instructions without being authoritarian. People are more likely to willingly carry out requests if they are framed as questions.

Can you imagine yourself using this approach to become more influential?

Selectional restriction violation

This is a sentence which attributes human intelligence, feelings and behaviours to inanimate objects.

"This book has the power to change your life."

Ambiguities

There are a number of different types of ambiguity.

- **Phonological**: Words that sound alike but have different meanings – such as here and hear.
- **Syntactic**: It's not possible to tell the exact meaning of the words in the context e.g. "selling salespeople can be easy". Does it mean it's easy to sell salespeople or easy to sell to salespeople or can salespeople be described as easy?
- **Scope**: The context does not make it clear to what a verb or modifier applies e.g. "Speaking to you as someone who has studied the language of influence...". Who has studied it – you or me?
- **Punctuation**: This can take the form of a run-on sentence where the first word of the second sentence is the same as the last word of the first sentence but you don't pause.

"Hand me your watch how quickly you go into a trance."

You can also have unexpected pauses in a sentence which don't follow the normal rules of punctuation and you can have rambling or incomplete sentences - all of which ultimately force the listener to 'mind read'.

"Would you like to read this now or...?"

Voice Intonation and Embedded Commands

The way you use your voice can have a big impact in the way your message is interpreted.

So it's important to learn how to use it most effectively.

There are three different voice intonations that are important.

- If your voice goes up at the end of a sentence, what you are saying is heard as a question. This is fine if you are asking a question but if you use this pattern too much, it sounds like you are questioning everything you are saying and comes across as incongruent.

- If your voice stays consistent throughout the sentence, this is seen as a statement.

- If the tonality of your voice goes down and the pitch decreases at the end of the sentence, this is seen as a command or instruction. This is an important factor in hypnotic communication.

The most powerful combination is the syntax of a question delivered using command tonality. In this case, the conscious mind hears a question but the unconscious mind hears a command.

There are two types of suggestion you need to be aware of.

- **Direct suggestion**: This is where you provide information that is evaluated by the conscious mind before making a decision. For example, a statement like 'Write this down' is a clear command and one that allows you to choose whether to do it or not.

41

- **Indirect suggestion**: This is where it is presented in a way that is not evaluated by the conscious mind but is taken on board by the unconscious mind. For example: "I'm wondering if you'll write this down and remember it when you need to."

If this is delivered with a command tonality it is taken unconsciously as a suggestion.

One of the most powerful ways to use your voice is by delivering 'embedded commands'. This is where you vary the pace or volume of your words to draw attention to particular elements.

For example, the phrase "I don't know whether you will want to buy this today" is heard consciously as a statement.

However if you put a slight emphasis on the words **buy this today**, it will be heard as a command.

You need to be realistic though and don't think that people are going to automatically dig out their credit cards when they hear this command. It is a subtle effect that builds up over time.

You can embed commands in writing by using a slightly different typeface but it works better when the change is subtle and not too obvious.

Influence in Action: Hypnotic Language

Here are some practical examples of how to use hypnotic language in different settings.

As you read through the list, think about some further examples and add them to each category.

For each pattern you create, consider the context in which you will use it and also decide your purpose or intended outcome in using it.

Mind reading

I can tell you're not happy
I know you came here for a reason
You already know this
I'm sure you've heard this before
I know what you're going to say
You'll be annoyed about this
You're going to enjoy this
I can tell you've had a difficult day
We know what you'll say when you hear this
I know you'll have read this in the handouts
You'll probably not like this
I bet you're going to love this
I'm sure you've felt this way before
I'm sure you don't mind if I do it like this
I realize you'll already have seen this
I can see you don't like this
I know you always like these
You're sitting there thinking that I'm crazy
You're enjoying learning these patterns
You'll love me for teaching you this

43

Now create your own examples. Think about how the pattern works, the context of the situation, and the outcome you want.

Lost Performative

It's really good that you say that

It's the best way

It's great that you can change

That's good

It's a bad idea to do that

It's important to say this

One doesn't need to

It's better to say so now

You're wrong about that

It's best to get it over with

It's perfect

It's fantastic to do this

It's wonderful

It's good to say what you think

We'll do what's right

No-one should do that

It was better before

That wasn't a good idea

It's worse if you don't

Nobody does it better

Your examples.

Cause and effect

As you listen to me, you'll see why our offer is right for you

If you come with me, you'll have a great time

As you sit there, you're already starting to feel better

Don't do that unless you want to...

After you've been you'll never be the same again

If you are here, then you are ready

Reading this will change your life

You can hear the music and it makes you feel relaxed

As you continue to read these patterns you'll become an expert

When you do this you'll make money

As you wait there you'll feel more excited

Waiting there makes you feel more excited

If you wait there, you'll feel more excited

Your examples.

Complex equivalence

Your questions show you're already seeing the benefits

Just by being here, you've shown you're ready to change

You relax a little more as you breathe out

Practicing regularly makes you an expert

Keeping your old furniture means nothing has changed

Having read all these examples means you understand it already

You've been practicing all week so now you can do it

Having seen me do it means you can do it yourself

You've done it before so you can do it again

Learning this one technique means you are a master

You're asking great questions so you already understand it perfectly

Just wearing the uniform makes you confident

Your examples.

Universal quantifiers

Everyone doing this is getting great results

Nobody's perfect

You already have everything

All the evidence points to this

Anyone can learn this

Everything will be taken into account

Everyone knows this is true

None of these works

All of these work

No-one knows everything

There is always more to do

All the people did this

Every person is happy

Each time is the same

There is always another

Everybody is an expert

No people have done this properly

Your examples.

Presuppositions

You can go through this process even more easily now

You're seeing the situation differently now

You are changing all the time

How many other ways can you succeed?

You'll make even more money next week

You'll find it even faster the next time

It's even easier with practice

You'll find it even more relaxing next time

You'll go into an even deeper trance later

You've already changed

You'll be able to do it even better

Now you'll find it easy to come up with more examples

Your examples.

Modal operators

You must be aware

You should know it's OK to do this

You can change today

You may be able to discover

You could easily find

You can trust yourself to do this

You have to make it happen

You may discover something new

You might find it's easier than you think

You shouldn't find this difficult

It's possible to do it easily

You could think of more

It's necessary to make the change

It had to be said

I must do it now

Your examples.

Nominalisation

Better communications will improve the understanding of everyone

Tell me how it affects your feelings

If you have trust in the process things will improve

It can have a positive impact on behaviour

This is a demonstration of your achievement

There will be change in your relationships

It's time to trust your intuitions

This will affect your thoughts about it

You'll find your desires will change

It comes down to your decision

This is an important learning

People will show you a lot of respect

Your examples.

Unspecified verbs

I was wondering

You may remember

You could even enjoy

Notice how easily

You could discover

You will be learning

You can notice

You will continue

Just let go

You will realise

You'll begin to feel

It's easy

You'll soon learn

You may be thinking

You'll quickly understand

Your examples.

Tag questions

You've already decided, haven't you?

You could try again, couldn't you?

You can do this now, can't you?

You'll be able to do this, won't you?

You do it better than anyone else, don't you now?

You haven't done that yet, have you?

It's so easy that way, isn't it?

We're going to do it this time, aren't we?

You would like to do this, would you not?

It's so much better this way, don't you think?

You can be very successful at this. And you can, can you not?

You won't let that happen, will you?

You are going to do this, are you not?

Your examples.

Lack of referential index

You can easily see

You have and you know it

Just let it go now

That's the way

It makes people change

You may not know it

One can, you know

Now you've got it

Please help

You'll notice the feeling

It would help

You've already done it

Your examples.

Comparative deletions

This is more or less the right time

You will enjoy it more

You are even more relaxed

He's doing it better now

It's easier to do this

You'll understand this better

Sooner or later you'll realise

You're going deeper into trance

It's harder this way

It's more or less the right way

You're on a higher level

One way is better

It's worse now

Your examples.

Pacing current experience

As you look at this chart

As you sit here with me

As you breathe in and out

While we are all here

As you get started

As you read these words

While you listen tot the traffic outside

As the rain falls

While we wait for the results

As you think about what this means

As you study this carefully, you'll notice

As you start to fall asleep

Your examples.

Double binds

Do you want to start next month or immediately?

Shall we go to the film tonight or on Saturday?

Will you make the change now or after you've had some sleep?

Either this week or next week

When you fall asleep or when you wake up

Take all the time you want to do this in the next 10 minutes

Shall we cover it at the meeting or by telephone?

Would you like a medium one or a large one?

Do you want it by post or by courier?

Do you want to pay for 6 sessions or 12?

Right now or after lunch

Tuesday or Thursday

Your examples.

Extended quotes

One of our clients was telling me that he'd had feedback from his sales team that the customers were saying this was the best service they'd ever had.

John was telling me that his wife has a friend who has faced problems like this and her doctor had told her that it was a very common situation.

A friend of mine had suffered this problem for years and her husband had asked a therapist what they should do and he said it was all about making the commitment to change.

A few years ago, I heard this story about an old man who'd been to visit a guru in the East and he'd shared with him everything that had been handed down by his father before him. He said you just need to do this once very day.

Bill has just come back from speaking at a conference and someone asked him a question about why so many people were getting great results. He said that everyone who tried this found their lives changed virtually overnight.

When I was on holiday with Jo, she was telling me about someone she knew whose mother had visited the same place before and she said it was great value for money

Your examples.

Utilisation

Client: This seems expensive.

Response: That's right. It seems expensive because I haven't yet shown you how you can get it at a special price.

Client: I don't think he likes me.

Response: That's right. You don't think he likes you because you haven't focused on all the nice things he said.

Client: I'll never be able to do this.

Response: That's right. You'll never be able to do this until you make this one change in the way you are approaching it.

Client: This is too difficult

Response: That's right. You think it's difficult because I haven't yet told you about the one step you need to take to make it easy.

Client: It doesn't seem to be working.

Response: That's right. It doesn't seem to be working because you've only been doing it for a few days. After a week, you'll see a big difference.

Your examples.

Conversational postulates

Does it sound like this would make you a lot of money?

Can you imagine us doing this together?

Wouldn't you just like to relax now?

Can you sign this?

Would it be all right to make that much?

Can you think about this?

Does this look like a good investment?

Can you see this working?

How easy would this be?

Wouldn't you like to try this?

Wouldn't it be great to have this now?

Would you mind just trying it for a few days?

Your examples.

Selectional restriction violation

The report said

These flowers can tell you something

This chair can tell some great stories of success

My heart tells me

Walls have ears

Listen to your body

Your pen knows the answer

That hurt my wallet

The budget won't allow it

The car will happily make the journey

Just listen to what the wind tells you

The windows love to be washed

Your examples.

Ambiguities

Speaking to you as an expert in finance

Thinking about this as a reasonable person

Why don't you look at your watch my hand drop deeper into trance

He went red as he read the report

He could bear to see the bare facts

She couldn't wait to lose weight

The fighting mean and women

The worrying noises and thoughts

They were visiting relatives

She was your love but did you love her?

As you hear more examples, write them right here

Annoying people

Your examples.

Example using all the hypnotic patterns together

Pattern	
Mind reading	*I know that you've been thinking about this*
Lost performative	*And that's a very good thing*
Cause and effect	*Because if you start using this system, you'll be able to sell faster*
Complex equivalence	*And faster sales are bigger profits*
Universal quantifiers	*Everyone agrees*
Presuppositions	*You'll be able to get even better results*
Modal operators	*You could easily find*
Nominalisation	*The changes that are made*
Unspecified verbs	*Will work*
Tag questions	*Couldn't you?*
Lack of referential index	*You'll see lot happening*
Comparative deletions	*It's better like that*
Pacing current experience	*As you review this proposal now*

Double binds	*It's a question of deciding whether to start today or next week*
Extended quotes	*Your sales manager was saying that his team were complaining that one of your major competitors was boasting about what a great investment this system is*
Utilisation	*The only reason you've not already decided to order is that I've not shown you the special deal that I've put together*
Conversational postulates	*Can you see how much money you could make if you order now?*
Selectional restriction violation	*The numbers tell you it's an easy decision*
Ambiguities	*As someone with an interest in the future of the company, I'm sure you can see that*

Practical Example: Opening a speech

It's wonderful to be here today.

You know, this event is the best. It's so much better.

I know you're ready to discover a few secrets that will help you earn more money quickly. Just by being here, you've already shown that you've got what it takes to get to the next level.

It's a good thing to get more learning at every opportunity. And today you've already learned more than you realise. Haven't you?

It's quite possible that what I'm going to share with you will help you earn so much more. And that would be a very good thing. I'm sure you'll agree.

Will you implement all of these ideas today or will you wait until tomorrow?

You'll find my presentation today has everything you need. And as you take notes, you'll find that you notice how easy it all is.

Everyone thinks that.

So now that you're ready, let's start to change.

Practical Example: Covering letter for a report

I know you've got many questions about how this proposal will work and that's why we've written this report. We know it's important.

If you don't have time to read all the detail, almost everyone finds they get a good understanding of what's involved by reading the short summary at the start. It's possible that's all you'll need.

Reading the summary will give you confidence in how the plans are going to work.

For those who need a detailed knowledge, there's more information in the full report included.

I'm sure you'll find that everything you need to know is either in the brief introduction or in the full report.

In taking time to read this, you're showing your commitment to the future success of the business and that alone will help make sure it works.

I believe you'll enjoy discovering the potential.

Practical Example: sales letter

Why Almost Everyone Makes This Business Mistake...

... And How You Can Avoid It

If you run your own business, you've had moments when you wonder, haven't you?

When you wonder how you'll get it all done.

I bet if someone could give you an extra hour a day, you'd take it.

So let me ask you – would you prefer an extra one hour a day or an extra two hours?

The truth is you've got more time than you realize.

But the fact is most business owners only have an hour or two of productive time a day. And that's bad.

Yet if someone showed you how to uncover an extra hour or two a day, you'd easily increase your profits. Wouldn't you?

Change like this is not only possible, it's easy.

Let me show you how.

6. The Secret of Unconscious Communication: How to Make Sure Your Message Meets No Resistance

One of the most powerful ways of bypassing conscious resistance to your message is to present it in the form of a story or metaphor.

Stories are part of our everyday communication but often we use them without a clear idea of what they are meant to achieve.

Metaphors are simply stories with a purpose – where you want people to relate the story to their own situation to lead them to change their behaviour in some way or to take a particular action.

Metaphors can be shallow – where it is very obvious to the person reading or listening to it how the story applies to them – or they can be deep – where it is not consciously obvious how the story applies to them.

> **"Stories are part of our everyday communication. Metaphors are simply stories with a purpose"**

An example of a **shallow metaphor** would be telling someone who was facing a challenge a story about someone who had battled against difficult odds to be successful.

A famous example of a **deep metaphor** was when Milton Erickson was asked to give help to a man who was suffering pain from cancer. The man was an enthusiastic gardener so when Erickson told him a story about feeding and caring for tomato plants, he just became absorbed in the story.

But the underlying purpose of the story was to plant ideas in his unconscious mind about caring for his own health. After hearing the story the man began to experience less pain and feel more comfortable.

Presenting your information in the form of a story creates less resistance and makes the message more likely to be accepted.

For example if you tell a story about how one of your clients has had their life changed as a result of your work, it is much more readily accepted than you telling them how great you are.

The value of metaphors can be enhanced by running a few different metaphors together as a series of stories.

The way this works is that you start telling one metaphor and then move on to the next one before you have finished the second. You can do this with a few stories.

This process is sometimes known as 'nested loops' or 'embedded metaphors' and is particularly useful in coaching sessions and presentations. We've included an example at the end of this section.

The fact that you have not finished the story makes the unconscious mind curious to know what has happened. But at the same time, you get absorbed in the new story.

This is consistent with the way people normally tell stories – they start one and never quite finish it. But they don't do this consciously and then they normally don't actually finish off the stories.

Then later on – after the main content of your presentation or coaching session – you 'close off' the metaphors by finishing off each of the stories in the reverse order from which you started them.

Influence in Action: Metaphors

Here are some examples of how to use metaphors in different practical settings. Add some examples of your own in different contexts.

Business

A firm of accountants in Birmingham installed this system just under a year ago. They'd previously had to pay thousands a month to get this service. But after using this for just three months, they we able to stop paying any money to outside suppliers and they found they covered the cost in less than four months. Not only have they saved money but it's actually helped them attract five new clients as well.

Relationships

Robert was telling me that his relationship was going really badly a few months ago. He was spending very little time with his wife and they were not talking about things. Somehow they both found the time to go to this resort in Ireland for a couple of weeks and he was telling me how much it had changed everything. They came back completely refreshed with their marriage re-energised. They're now going to renew their vows.

Therapy

Mike's doctor told him that he had to give up smoking but he's been pretty stubborn and really didn't want to do anything about it. He said it was too late to change. The one thing that made him change his mind was his visit to the local hospital when he could see for himself some of the X-rays and some of the ways people were suffering. As soon as he could see for himself how other people were being affected, he realized it was never too late to stop.

Influence in Action: Nested Loops / Embedded Metaphors

This is a short example of how you can weave a number of stories – three in the example – to build and retain interest. Note how the transitions between them are smooth but each leaves us wanting to know more.

*I was recently eating in a quiet restaurant in the country and was stunned when Simon Cowell of Britain's Got Talent walked in. As he walked past my table, he asked how the salmon was. I told him it was the best I'd ever tasted and I **told him something else** as well.*

*In fact, I'd once had even better salmon in a restaurant in Edinburgh. That one was something special as **I'd won the prize** in a competition.*

*I was amazed that Prince Charles was staying in our hotel and I'll **never forget** what the doorman told me the next day.*

[Main content of presentation here]

That morning in Edinburgh, I asked the doorman if he'd met the Prince and what he told me next was amazing. It turns out that Prince Charles had been in the same hotel over a year ago and he remembered the doorman's name and asked after his children.

That was a great lesson to me because even though I'd won that prize to Edinburgh in a public speaking competition, I realised how much better results I'd get by remembering something about every individual I meet.

I wonder if Simon Cowell will remember that I told him I was going to enter his talent competition next year. I hope he enjoyed the salmon as much as I did.

7.   A Question of Influence: How Asking the Right Questions Makes the Difference Between Failure and Success in Communication

As we've mentioned in previous sections, the statements people make represent only part of what they are thinking.

So one of the key skills in influential communication is using questions to get a clearer picture of what someone means by a particular statement.

Earlier we noted that people tend to delete, distort or generalize information when they process it in their mind and this is reflected in their communication.

So the purpose of questions is to replace the information they have deleted, distorted or generalized so that we can understand them better.

The model for this from NLP is called the Meta Model and it is the reverse of the Milton Model that we previously looked at.

- The Milton Model moves communication to a more generalized level to generate trance and to increase the potential for agreement.

- The Meta Model makes communication more specific so that we can get a clearer idea of what somebody is thinking.

So here are the Meta Model questions in each category.

In these examples, we show the original statement and the response required to uncover the missing information.

Distortions

- Mind Reading: Claiming to know what the other person is thinking.

  "You don't like me."

  "How do you know I don't like you?"

- Lost Performative: A value judgement where the person doing the judging is not specified.

  "It's a bad thing to be persuasive."

  "Who says it's bad?" "How do you know it's bad?"

- Cause and Effect: A statement that claims one thing causes another.

  "You make me angry."

  "How specifically does what I'm doing cause you to choose to feel angry?"

- Complex Equivalence: Where two experiences are equated.

  "He's always shouting at me, he doesn't like me."

  "Have you ever shouted at someone you liked?"

- Presuppositions

  "If my boss knew how much I hated it, he wouldn't do it."

  There are three Presuppositions in this sentence:

  (1) I hate something

  "What specifically do you hate about it?"

  (2) My boss acts in some way

  "How is he acting?"

  (3) My boss doesn't know I hate it.

"How do you know he doesn't know?"

Generalisations

- Universal Quantifiers: Generalizations such as all, every, never, everyone, nobody.

  "She never pays attention to me."

  Find Counter Examples. "Never?"

- Modal Operators

  o Modal Operators of Necessity: should, shouldn't, must, must not, have to, need to, it is necessary.

  "I have to go there."

  "What would happen if you didn't?"

  o Modal Operators of Possibility (Or Impossibility.) can/can't, will/won't, may/may not, possible/impossible.

  "I can't tell him the truth."

  "What prevents you?" "What would happen if you did?"

Deletions

- Nominalizations: Process words which have been frozen in time, making them nouns.

  "There is no communication here."

  "Who's not communicating what to whom?"

- Unspecified Verbs:

  "He annoyed me."

  "How, specifically?"

- Simple Deletions

  "I am unhappy."

  "About what/whom?"

- Lack of Referential Index: Fails to specify a person or thing.

  "They don't listen to me."

  "Who, specifically, doesn't listen to you?"

- Comparative Deletions: The person or thing to which the comparison is made is not specified as in good, better, best, worst, more, less, most, and least.

  "He's a better manager."

  "Better at what?" "Compared to who, what?

Influence in Action: Meta Model Questions

Here are some examples of how to use Meta Model questions to respond to statements that people make indicating limits in their thinking.

As you read through the examples, think about some further examples and add them to each category.

Mind Reading

You don't like me	How do you know I don't like you?
I know you're angry	What am I doing that makes you think I'm angry?
You think I'm stupid	What exactly do I do to make you believe that?
He didn't enjoy it	What specifically did he do that makes you think he didn't enjoy it?
You'll hate me for this	What makes you sure that I'll hate it?
You've probably seen this before	Why do you think I've seen it before?
I can see you don't like this	What makes you think that?
You'll love this	What exactly will I love about it?
I bet you won't do this	How do you know I won't?
I know what you're going to say?	How can you be sure?

Your examples

Lost Performative

It's a bad thing to be persuasive	How do you know it's bad?
It's good to learn this	Who says it's good?
It's better to say so now	Why is it better?
That's good	What exactly is good about it?

70

That wasn't a good idea	Who says it wasn't?
It's perfect	What makes it perfect?
You're wrong	Says who?
It was better before	What specifically was better about it?
Do the right thing	Who says what is right?
Nobody does it better	What do you mean by better?

Your examples

Cause and Effect

You make me angry	How specifically does what I'm doing cause you to choose to feel angry?
If I do that I'll fail	What exactly will happen if you do it?
Sitting here makes me tired	Do you only get tired when you sit here?
As I listen to you, I get more annoyed	What exactly is making you annoyed?
If you do what I say, you'll make a lot of money	Are there other ways to make money?
Waiting makes me angry	What specifically about waiting makes you angry
As you go on doing that, you'll find yourself getting more relaxed	Can I stop doing it and still relax?
When you do that I get very excited	What else makes you excited?
If you do that again, I'll leave	If I never do it again does that mean you will never leave?
Don't read this unless you want to be rich	Do I only need to read this to become rich?

Your examples

Complex Equivalence

He's always shouting at me, he doesn't like me.	Have you ever shouted at someone you liked?
The fact that you do that means you are tired	Could it mean anything else?
Continuing to do that means you don't want to succeed	Has anyone done it this way and succeeded?
Your questions show that you're not interested	Does asking questions not show that I'm interested?
Practicing once a week means you don't want to be the best	What if I practice for five times longer than everyone else?
As you breathe out you get more relaxed	So if I just breathe out all the time, will I get very relaxed?
Just by being here, you've shown you are ready to buy	What if being here has made me change my mind?
As you always ignore what I say, you obviously don't take me seriously	If I'm ignoring what you say I must be listening and taking you seriously.
You've never done it before so don't expect to do it now	Isn't there a first time for everything?
As you've waited until now, you clearly don't want to do this	What if I've waited for the right moment and that moment is now

Your examples

Presuppositions

If my boss knew how much I hated it, he wouldn't do it	What specifically do you hate about it?
	How is he acting?
	How do you know he doesn't know?
If you realized how much I loved you, you would buy me flowers every day	How do you know I don't know that?
	Is buying flowers the only way to show that?
	What if I buy them only every second day?
If you change the way you work, you'll be much happier	How do you know I'm not happy?
	What exactly do I need to change?
If you practice more often, you'll make more money	How do you know how often I practice?
	How do you know I want to make more money?

Your examples

Universal Quantifiers

She never pays attention to me	Can you think of just one time she did?
You always do that	Has there ever been a time when I didn't?
Everybody knows	Is there anyone who doesn't know?
Nobody has ever done this	Has everybody tried?
We always argue	Is there anything we don't argue

	about?
Everyone is laughing	Is there anyone who isn't laughing?
You blame me for everything	Is there anything I haven't blamed you for?
There is nothing left to do	Is it possible to do anything else?
Everything is perfect	Is there nothing that can be improved?
No-one likes our new products	Are there any of the products that somebody does like?

Your examples

Modal Operators

I have to go there	What would happen if you didn't?
I can't tell him the truth	What prevents you?
I need to do it	Who says?
You should know this already	How should I know?
You can do this	How exactly can I do it?
You shouldn't do that	Who says?
You mustn't go there	What will happen if I do?
It's impossible	How do you know?
You have to stop it	Who says?
It's not necessary to do that	What would happen if I did?

Your examples

Nominalisations

There is no communication here	Who's not communicating what to whom?
It affects my feelings	What does it make you feel?
I don't like the process	What is being done that you don't like?
There are many useful learnings	What exactly will I learn?
I trust my intuition	What is your intuition telling you?
The relationships are poor	How exactly are people relating badly to one another?
I'm not achieving my desires	What specifically do you desire that you are not achieving?
It is a difficult decision	What exactly do you have to decide?
I'm disappointed with your lack of achievement	What precisely do you want me to achieve?
My thoughts are very negative	What exactly are you thinking that has a negative effect?

Your examples

Unspecified Verbs

He annoyed me	How specifically?
You made me	What exactly did I make you do?
You may remember	Remember what exactly?
You will be learning	What exactly will I be learning?
I was wondering	What specifically were you wondering?
You'll begin to feel	What precisely will I feel?
You may be thinking	What will I be thinking about?
You'll soon understand	What exactly will I understand?

It's easy	What exactly is easy about it?
Just do it	What exactly should I do?

Your examples

Simple Deletions

I'm unhappy	About what?
I'm angry	What exactly are you angry about?
I'm bored	Why are you bored?
He's disappointed	What exactly is he disappointed about?
She's worried	What's worrying her?
I'm nervous	What makes you nervous?
She's in a panic	What's making her panic?
He's excited	What exactly is making him excited?
I'm confused	What have you not understood yet?
She's upset	What precisely is upsetting her?

Your examples

Lack of Referential Index

They don't listen to me	Who, specifically, doesn't listen to you?
It makes people change	What exactly makes people change? In what way do they change?
It would help	What exactly would help? How would it help?
You've done it	What precisely have I done?
You'll notice the feeling	What exactly will I feel?

One can, you know	What exactly can one do?
	How does one do it?
Please help	What help do you need exactly
You can see it easily	What exactly can I see?
You know already	Know what exactly?
I haven't got it	What haven't you got yet?

Your examples

Comparative Deletions

He's a better manager	Compared to whom?
It's harder like that	What exactly makes it harder?
It's too expensive	Compared to what?
This is the best way	Who says so?
It's worse that way	Worse for what?
You are less relaxed	Less than what?
This is easier to follow	What makes it easier?
It's less enjoyable	Why is it less enjoyable?
	Less enjoyable than what?
This is a faster way	Faster than what?
This is better	Better than what?

Your examples

8.   Winning Every Argument: The Process That Virtually Guarantees to Change Minds and Get the Outcome You Want

The language system known as Sleight of Mouth patterns is one of the most powerful methods of changing someone's beliefs conversationally.

Often our beliefs are held within a frame of reference (which may or may not be conscious) that creates very restrictive thinking.

To loosen up this restrictive thinking we need to use a process of reframing to create a different perspective on the situation.

This applies whether we are looking at a business situation where you are trying to influence someone to your point of view or whether it is a coaching/therapy situation where we are trying to help someone overcome a problem.

The immediate purpose of reframing is not necessarily to change their mind or resolve the problem. It may be to "soften up" the situation and open them up to other possibilities.

The Sleight of Mouth patterns are a very powerful reframing tool developed by Robert Dilts one of the world's leading NLP experts.

His work involved modelling people such as Karl Marx, Milton Erickson, Abraham Lincoln, Jesus and Mohandas Gandhi. He also studies the persuasion skills of Richard Bandler – one of the co-creators of NLP who was renowned for his ability to win any argument.

The name was taken from the phrase "sleight of hand" which normally refers to the magician's skill in making things happen which seem to be impossible.

The aim of the patterns is to help people understand the process of persuasion and influence and to enable them to duplicate the skills of master persuaders.

Dilts' original work has also been supplemented by others who later added more patterns.

Sleight of mouth patterns work by challenging existing beliefs so that they are easier to change.

Beliefs are typically expressed in one of two forms:

- **Complex equivalence**: A equals or means B

- **Cause and effect**: A causes, leads to or results in B

If the belief is not expressed as a complex equivalence or cause-effect assertion – for example someone saying "I don't like this", we need to find out more by asking some questions.

As is normally the case with successful persuasion and influence, the purpose of sleight of mouth is not to attack the person or the belief. The key is to help them look at the situation from another perspective so that they reach a different conclusion.

We'll look first at a description of the key patterns and then cover some examples which will make it easier to understand and apply.

79

Here are the 14 Sleight of Mouth patterns originally identified by Dilts that can be applied to challenge a statement of someone's belief.

- **Intention**: You put the attention on the purpose or intention behind the belief. You can do this by highlighting their positive intent or by challenging the negative intent.

- **Redefining**: Substituting a new word for one of the words in the belief statement that has a similar meaning but a different implication.

- **Consequence**: Directing attention to an effect (positive or negative) of the belief which results in the belief being challenged.

- **Chunk Down**: Breaking the belief down into smaller pieces such that it challenges the generalization defined by the belief.

- **Chunk Up**: Generalise an element of the belief to a larger classification that changes the relationship defined by the belief.

- **Analogy / Metaphor**: Finding a relationship analogous to that defined by the belief which challenges the generalization defined by the belief.

- **Change Frame Size**: Re-evaluating the implication of the belief in the context of a larger (or a smaller) perspective or to a longer (or shorter) time frame.

- **Another Outcome**: Switching to a different goal than that implied by the belief in order to challenge its relevancy.

- **Model of the World**: Re-evaluate the belief from the perspective of a different model of the world.

- **Reality strategy**: Re-evaluate the belief allowing for the fact that beliefs arise from individual perceptions. Ultimately, this is about asking how they know their belief is true, or what aspects of the belief really are the issue.

- **Counter Example**: Finding an 'exception to the rule' where their statement would not be true – which causes the belief that underlies the statement to be questioned.

- **Hierarchy of Criteria**: Re-evaluate the belief based on more important criteria or values than those addressed by the belief, suggesting something more important they should be considering.

- **Apply to Self**: Turn the comment back on itself by evaluating it according to the criteria defined by the belief.

- **Meta frame**: Challenge the basis behind the belief, rather than the belief. In other words, establish a belief about the belief to suggest that their belief presupposes something.

Example: Sleight of Mouth Patterns

The best way to understand how Sleight of Mouth patters work – so that you can use them for yourself – is to see some examples.

We've included some examples in the next section. One is in a business context and the other is in therapy.

Influence in Action: Sleight of Mouth Patterns

Example in Business Context

Here's an example of using each of these patterns addressed to the following common objection faced in business.

I can't hire you because your fees are too high

This is a complex equivalence where A means B. we can therefore apply some of our reframes to the A side and to the B side.

- **Intention**: I admire your desire to get the best value for money and you'll find our fees are well worth the investment

- **Redefining**: Our fees are great value because our service includes so much

- **Consequence**: If you always buy based on price you'll often end up making bad choices

- **Chunk Down**: Which precise part of our service is too expensive for you?

- **Chunk Up**: We were going to charge ten times as much when we realised how much was included

- **Analogy / Metaphor**: If you were staying in a hotel would you always choose the cheapest?

- **Change Frame Size**: That might be true if you had to pay the fees for 20 years but we'll finish in six months

- **Another Outcome**: Cost is never the real issue the question is whether you want to get this sorted quickly

- **Model of the World**: Many of our clients said that at first until they discovered how much money we saved them

- **Reality strategy**: How do you know our fees are high?

- **Counter Example**: We used to charge less but people didn't take our advice seriously

- **Hierarchy of Criteria**: We believe it's important to employ only the best consultants so we have to pay them more

- **Apply to Self**: That's a very expensive attitude. It will cost you more in the long-run

- **Meta frame**: That's only because you haven't realized how much you are losing each day you don't hire us

Example in Therapy Context

Here's an example of using each of these patterns addressed to the following common situation faced in therapy.

The fact I've had this problem so long means I'll never get rid of it

This is a complex equivalence where A means B. we can therefore apply some of our reframes to the A side and to the B side.

- **Intention**: What does holding on to this problem allow you to avoid?

- **Redefining**: Holding on to the problem a long time doesn't mean it isn't easy to get rid of

- **Consequence**: If you think that way you'll never be able to change anything

- **Chunk Down**: When exactly did you start having this problem?

- **Chunk Up**: So do you think this problem will exist even after you're gone?

- **Analogy / Metaphor**: My friends had lived in the same house for 40 years and then they moved to live at the seaside and they're life has been renewed

- **Change Frame Size**: So if you'd had the problem for twice as long, would it be twice as hard to get rid of?

- **Another Outcome**: Getting rid of the problem isn't the issue here. The question is whether you want to be stubborn

- **Model of the World**: Lots of people had the problem much longer than you and then got rid of it overnight

- **Reality strategy**: How do you know it's hard to get rid of the problem?

- **Counter Example**: Do you know anyone who ha a problem for even longer and still managed to get rid of it?

- **Hierarchy of Criteria**: Is there some reason why holding on to the problem is better than getting rid of it?

- **Apply to Self**: Have you had that belief for longer than you've had the problem?

- **Meta frame**: That's only because you haven't realized how quickly this process works

9. Summary of the Keys to the Language of Influence

Here is a quick summary of the keys to the language of influence that we've covered in this book.

* **We filter information in the mind to make it easier to manage**
  The human mind is subjected to huge volumes of information every second but has an inbuilt filter mechanism to help it cope.

  One of the key parts of this filter process is that we sort information by deleting, distorting and generalizing based on our past experience.

  This same process can assist and hinder communication so it's important to understand it.

* **We communicate using all of the senses**
  Communication is not only through words but involves all five senses – sight, sound, touch, taste and smells.

* **Our words represent only part of the meaning**
  Our words convey only part of the meaning of communication. The words we choose demonstrate 'presuppositions' – these are the beliefs that we need to hold in order for the words to be true.

  > *"When the sentence involves a lot of presuppositions, it's normally harder to convince someone of your message."*

  When the sentence involves a lot of presuppositions, it will normally be harder to convince someone of your message.

- **Communication that is more generic can achieve agreement faster**

  The Milton Model is a communication tool that allows you to make your language more generic so that it is easier to achieve rapport and easier to reach agreement.

- **Metaphors break down conscious resistance**

  Metaphors are stories with a purpose that can communicate directly with the unconscious mind and the messages will be resisted less by the conscious mind.

- **Asking the right question can help improve communication**

  The Meta Model is a series of questions you can use to help clarify the meaning behind communication that is too general.

- **Knowing the right techniques can help you win any argument**

  The Sleight of Mouth patterns are a series of techniques you can use to help people see something differently and make it easier for them to change their minds.

10. Language Patterns of the World's Top Persuaders

One of the most persuasive people in the world right now is US President Barack Obama.

He is a master of delivery as his impact is driven partly by his powerful body language and careful use of gestures. But his language in important speeches is carefully chosen and very effective.

Just look at some of the patterns he uses in his election night victory speech in Detroit. Notice how some of his phrases combine several different patterns to maximum effect. We've highlighted some but you'll notice more.

Speech	Pattern example
If there is anyone out there who still doubts that America is a place where all things are possible	Universal Quantifier
who still wonders if the dream of our founders is alive in our time, who still questions the power of our democracy,	Nominalisation
tonight is your answer.	Nominalisation Utilisation Lost Performative
It's the answer told by lines that stretched around schools and churches in	Selectional Restriction Violation
numbers this nation has never seen, by people who waited three hours and four hours, many for the first time in their lives,	Universal Quantifier
because they believed that this time must be different,	Modal Operator (Necessity)
that their voices could be that difference.	Modal Operator (Possibility)

It's the answer spoken by… Americans who sent a message to the world that we have never been just a collection of individuals or a collection of red states and blue states. We are, and always will be, the United States of America.	Universal Quantifier
It's the answer that led those who've been told for so long	Cause & Effect
by so many to be cynical and fearful and doubtful about what we can achieve to put their hands on the arc of history	Modal Operator
and bend it once more toward the hope	Nominalisation
of a better day.	Lack of Referential Index
It's been a long time coming, but tonight,	Lost Performative Unspecified Verb
because of what we did on this date in this election at this defining moment	Cause and Effect
change has come to America.	Unspecified Verb Nominalisation
A little bit earlier this evening, I received an extraordinarily gracious call from Sen. McCain. Sen. McCain fought long and hard in this campaign. And he's fought even longer and harder for the country that he loves. He has endured sacrifices for America	Nominalisation
that most of us cannot begin to imagine.	Modal Operator
We are better off for the service rendered by this brave and selfless leader.	Comparative Deletion
. . . .	

To the best campaign team ever assembled in the history of politics you made this happen, and I am forever grateful for what you've sacrificed to get it done. But above all, I will never forget who this victory truly belongs to. It belongs to you. It belongs to you.	Lost Performative
I was never the likeliest candidate for this office. We didn't start with much money or many endorsements.	Lost Performative
This is your victory.	
And I know you didn't do this just to win an election. And I know you didn't do it for me.	Mind Read
You did it because you understand the enormity of the task that lies ahead. For even as we celebrate tonight,	Pacing Current Experience
we know the challenges that tomorrow will bring are the greatest of our lifetime -- two wars, a planet in peril, the worst financial crisis in a century.	Nominalisation
What began 21 months ago in the depths of winter cannot end on this autumn night.	Modal Operator
This victory alone is not the change we seek. It is only the chance for us to make that change.	Nominalisation
And that cannot happen if we go back to the way things were. It can't happen without you,	Modal Operators

without a new spirit of service, a new spirit of sacrifice.	Nominalisation
So let us summon a new spirit of patriotism, of responsibility, where each of us resolves to pitch in	Universal Quantifier
and work harder and look after not only ourselves but each other.	Lack of Referential Index
. . . .	
And to those Americans whose support I have yet to earn, I may not have won your vote tonight, but I hear your voices.	Utilisation
I need your help. And I will be your president, too.	Modal Operator
. . . .	
To those -- to those who would tear the world down: We will defeat you. To those who seek peace and security: We support you. And to all those who have wondered if America's beacon still burns as bright:	Unspecified verb
Tonight we proved once more that the true strength of our nation comes not from the might of our arms or the scale of our wealth, but from the enduring power of our ideals: democracy, liberty, opportunity and unyielding hope.	Nominalisations
That's the true genius of America: that America can change. Our union can be perfected.	Lack of Referential Index
What we've already achieved gives us hope for what we can and must achieve	Presupposition Modal Operators

tomorrow.	Universal Quantifier
This election had many firsts and many stories that will be told for generations. But one that's on my mind tonight's about a woman who cast her ballot in Atlanta. She's a lot like the millions of others who stood in line to make their voice heard in this election except for one thing: Ann Nixon Cooper is 106 years old. She was born just a generation past slavery; a time when there were no cars on the road or planes in the sky; when someone like her couldn't vote for two reasons -- because she was a woman and because of the colour of her skin.	Metaphor
And tonight, I think about all that she's seen throughout her century in America -- the heartache and the hope; the struggle and the progress;	Nominalisations
the times we were told that we can't, and the people who pressed on with that American creed:	Modal Operator
Yes we can.	Modal Operator Lack of Referential Index Unspecified Verb
. . . .	
And this year, in this election, she touched her finger to a screen, and cast her vote, because after 106 years in America, through the best of times and the darkest of hours, she knows how America can change.	Mind Read

Yes we can.	Modal Operator Lack of Referential Index Unspecified Verb
America, we have come so far. We have seen so much. But there is so much more to do.	Lack of Referential Index
So tonight, let us ask ourselves -- if our children should live to see the next century; if my daughters should be so lucky to live as long as Ann Nixon Cooper, what change will they see? What progress will we have made?	Conversational Postulate
This is our chance to answer that call. This is our moment. This is our time, to put our people back to work and open doors of opportunity for our kids; to restore prosperity and promote the cause of peace;	Nominalisations
to reclaim the American dream and reaffirm that fundamental truth, that, out of many, we are one;	Nominalisation
that while we breathe, we hope.	Complex Equivalence
And where we are met with cynicism and doubts and those who tell us that we can't, we will respond with that timeless creed that sums up the spirit of a people:	Cause & Effect
Yes, we can.	Modal Operator Lack of Referential Index Unspecified Verb

One of the most influential speakers in history is the wartime British Prime Minister, Winston Churchill

Many of his words have become etched on the minds of the generations that have followed but few recognise that many of his most famous phrases are powerful language patterns.

The following is an extract from his speech to the House of Commons the day he was elected prime minister – 13th May 1940.

At this point, he did not enjoy total support and he his task was to get parliament and the people behind him.

Speech	Pattern example
In this crisis I think I may be pardoned if I do not address the House at any length today, and I hope that any of my friends and colleagues or former colleagues who are affected by the political reconstruction will make all allowances for any lack of ceremony	Mind Read Lost Performance
with which it has been necessary to act.	Modal Operator
I say to the House as I said to ministers who have joined this government, I have nothing to offer	Universal Quantifier
but blood, toil, tears, and sweat.	Nominalisations
We have before us an ordeal of the most grievous kind.	Lack of Referential Index
We have before us many, many months of struggle and suffering.	Complex Equivalence Nominalisations Lack of Referential Index

You ask, what is our policy? I say it is to wage war by land, sea, and air. War with all our might and with all the strength God has given us,	Universal Quantifier
and to wage war against a monstrous tyranny	Metaphor
never surpassed in the dark and lamentable catalogue of human crime.	Universal Quantifier
That is our policy.	Nominalisation
You ask, what is our aim? I can answer in one word. It is victory. Victory at all costs - victory in spite of all terrors - victory, however long and hard the road may be,	Presupposition
for without victory there is no survival.	Complex Equivalence Universal Quantifier
Let that be realized. No survival for the British Empire, no survival for all that the British Empire has stood for, no survival for the urge, the impulse of the ages, that mankind shall move forward toward his goal.	Deletion
I take up my task in buoyancy and hope.	Metaphor
I feel sure that our cause will not be suffered to fail among men. I feel entitled at this juncture, at this time, to claim the aid of all and to say,	Mind Read
"Come then, let us go forward together	Unspecified Verb
with our united strength."	Universal Quantifier

11.   Using Your Mastery of Influence to Become More Successful

Learning the theory behind the language of influence is only the start of the story.

The real power of influence comes from making this knowledge and these patterns part of the way you communicate all the time so that you can always have a better chance of getting the outcome you want.

The only way to do that is to learn the patterns described here and practice them.

Often the best way to do that is to choose one at a time and focus on it for a day or two.

- Notice other people using it when they speak
- Look for examples of the patterns when you read newspapers and magazines
- Make up your own examples to add to those here
- Spend time reading great advertising and marketing pieces or watching powerful speeches – notice the patterns at work

However the most important thing to do is to make a habit of using them in your own written and spoken communication.

In the early days, you will have to practice very consciously. When you face a situation where you know you will need to use the advanced skills of influence, you will need to think carefully about which patterns to use.

The key is never to feel self-conscious about using these tools.

Other people will not notice that you sometimes don't get them right first time. It's a process of constant practice and improvement.

The more often you use the skills you have learned here, the more chance you have of getting the results you want.

Work through the different steps and figure out which combination will achieve the results you want.

> *"The more often you use the skills you have learned here, the more chance you have of getting the results you want."*

But, over time, as you integrate these patterns into you normal communication, you will naturally become a master of the language of influence.

You will be able to use these skills in many different situations, depending on your needs – such as:

- Make sales easily and comfortably
- Motivate your team
- Achieve the outcome you want with complaints and customer service issues
- Have more influence and impact at meetings
- Feel more confidence in your ability to get what you want
- Be an agent for change in your community
- Achieve promotion to higher levels at work

You'll soon discover that, as a master of the language of influence, there is not much you cannot achieve.

INDEX

You are invited to visit www.free-nlp.co.uk to discover a range of resources including CDs, DVDs and books on related subjects.

Training Excellence offers the highest standard in training, which includes:

NLP Diploma

NLP Practitioner

NLP Master Practitioner

Coaching Practitioner

Corporate Coaching

Hypnosis Practitioner

Hypnosis Master Practitioner

Public Speaking

We would like to thank you for purchasing this book and if you have any questions or would like to share your experiences of using NLP Language Patterns with us please email john@free-nlp.co.uk

Also download our free iPhone app, NLP Dictionary.

Kind regards

John